Barnyard GAMES & PUZZLES

100 Mazes, Word Games, Picture Puzzles, Jokes & Riddles, Brainteasers, and Fun Activities for Kids

Helene Hovanec & Patrick Merrell

Storey Publishing

The mission of Storey Publishing is to serve our customers by publishing practical information that encourages personal independence in harmony with the environment.

Edited by Lisa H. Hiley
Illustrations and design by Patrick Merrell
Art direction and cover design by Kent Lew
Production assistance by Kristy MacWilliams
Cover photograph by Digital Vision / Getty Images

The information in this book is true and complete to the best of our knowledge. All recommendations are made without guarantee on the part of the author or Storey Publishing. The author and publisher disclaim any liability in connection with the use of this information. For additional information please contact Storey Publishing, 210 MASS MoCA Way, North Adams, MA 01247.

Storey books are available for special premium and promotional uses and for customized editions. For further information, please call 1-800-793-9396.

Printed in the United States by Malloy
10 9 8 7 6 5 4 3 2 1

Dedicated to:

And a big thanks to:

CONTENTS

④ EVENING ROUNDUP

Tough Teasers to Show How Smart You Are
page 87

WELCOME!

INSTRUCTIONS

This book is divided into four sections that will take you through a day on the farm. The puzzles become more challenging as you go along, so you might want to start at the beginning and work your way through. Or you can pick and choose the ones that look like the most fun.

Before you start, have a look at the barnyard dictionary on page 113 to see if you know all the words that you might need to solve these puzzles. Here are a few other suggestions:

- Use a pencil in case you need to erase anything.
- You can do most of these puzzles on your own, but some are made for two people, so have a friend, parent, or brother or sister join in the fun on those ones.
- The answers start on page 117, and it's okay to peek if you need a hint.

Have a great time on the farm! Let's get going . . .

Cool! Instructions! Don't you just love instructions?

You've got to be kidding!

Boring.

Let's check out the next page.

MOVE IT

Move the letters listed below to the same-numbered spaces at the bottom of the page to find the first line from a familiar song. For example, A gets moved to spaces 5, 10, 14, 16, and 18.

LETTERS

A = 5, 10, 14, 16, 18
C = 6
D = 3, 7, 12, 15
F = 17
H = 13

L = 2, 11
M = 4, 20
N = 9
O = 1, 8
R = 19

THE SONG'S FIRST LINE:

$\overline{\quad}$ $\overline{\quad}$ $\overline{\quad}$　$\overline{\quad}$ $\overline{\quad}$ $\overline{\quad}$ $\overline{\quad}$ $\overline{\quad}$ $\overline{\quad}$ $\overline{\quad}$ $\overline{\quad}$ $\overline{\quad}$
1　2　3　　4　5　6　7　8　9　10　11　12

$\overline{\quad}$ $\overline{\quad}$ $\overline{\quad}$　$\overline{\quad}$　$\overline{\quad}$ $\overline{\quad}$ $\overline{\quad}$ $\overline{\quad}$
13　14　15　　16　　17　18　19　20

17

8 CHECK THIS OUT

Circle all the words with a ✔ in front of them.
Then read down to find a riddle and answer.

★WHY ✖WHEN ▼WHERE ✔WHAT ●WHO

✖DID ●DON'T ★WILL ▼WOULD ✔DO ■DIDN'T ✚COULD

✚BARN ●STALL ✔FARM ★MEADOW ✖STABLE ▼SILO

✔CATS ▼DOGS ■FROGS ✖RABBITS ●BUNNIES ✚HORSES

■DINE ✚MUNCH ●CHEW ★DRINK ✔EAT

▼IN ✔ON ■OUT ✖WITH ★OVER

✚THE ●AN ✔A ▼ANY ■SOME

●COLD ✖WINDY ✔HOT ★STORMY ▼RAINY

✔DAY? ✚NIGHT? ●MORNING? ✖AFTERNOON? ★EVENING?

✖RAT ▼FLEA ●RODENT ✔MICE ★LOCUST

★MILK ✔CREAM ▼YOGURT ●CHEESE

18

HORSE FOOD

Name each picture and write its first letter on the blank space. Then read the numbers from 1 to 8 to spell something that horses eat.

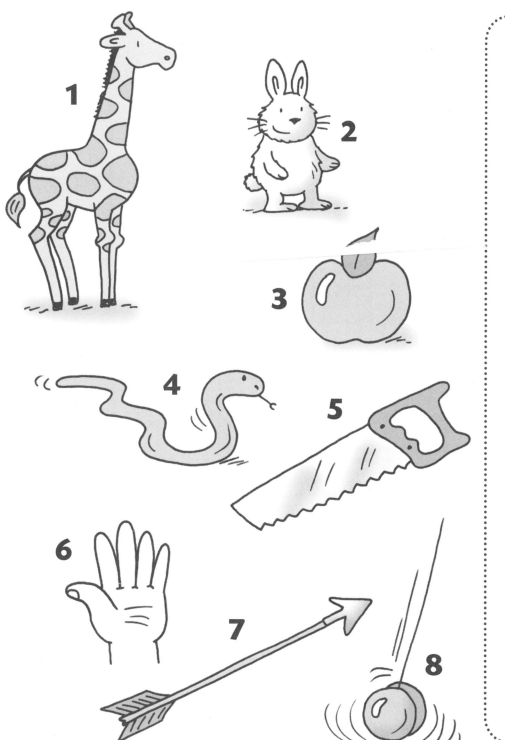

1. ____

2. ____

3. ____

4. ____

5. ____

6. ____

7. ____

8. ____

WHAT'S WRONG?

It looks like everything is wrong with this picture, doesn't it?
Actually there are only 10 things wrong — can you find them all?

11

What one word below means two different things — a male goat and a one-dollar bill? To find this word, cross off each word that is in both the top and the bottom box. The leftover word is the answer!

BABY	BACK	BAIT	BAKE	BALL
BAND	BANK	BUCK	BASE	BEAD
BEAK	BEAN	BEAR	BEAT	BECK
BELL	BEND	BALE	BIRD	BOAT
BOWL	BONE	BLUE	BARN	BARK

Read me the words from below, and I'll cross them off up above.

Alrighty! BACK, BABY . . .

BACK	BABY	BARN	BEAN	BECK	BASE
BEAR	BELL	BARK	BEAD	BIRD	BAIT
BEND	BAND	BALE	BOWL	BANK	BEAT
BAKE	BEAK	BALL	BOAT	BONE	BLUE

21

Quack!
Quack!

12 THREESIES

Cross off every letter that appears in the grid THREE times. Then put the leftover letters in the blank spaces below. Go from left to right and top to bottom to find the answer to this riddle:

What do you call a crate of ducks?

D	A	G	G	B	I	I	D
D	G	O	N	X	I	O	M
M	M	N	N	P	T	F	V
V	Q	P	P	T	T	V	U
Z	W	W	Y	Y	Y	Z	A
C	W	K	L	Z	E	J	J
J	L	L	R	H	H	H	S

Riddle answer:

— — — — — — — — — — — — — —

22

ORDER! ORDER!

Can you put these four pictures in order so that they make sense?
Write numbers from 1 to 4 in the circles.

WORM SQUIRM

START

After a hard day of tunneling in the cornfield, Squiggy could use a good rest in his comfy bed. Can you help him find the way to his bedroom?

END

SQUIGGY

SING ALONG

The letters in a popular game have been replaced by numbers. Look at the box to figure out what letter each number stands for. Write that letter on the blank space above the number. Then read the words to find the name of the game.

1 = A	2 = D	3 = E	4 = F
5 = H	6 = I	7 = L	8 = M
9 = N	10 = R	11 = T	

Answer:

$\overline{11}$ $\overline{5}$ $\overline{3}$ $\overline{4}$ $\overline{1}$ $\overline{10}$ $\overline{8}$ $\overline{3}$ $\overline{10}$

$\overline{6}$ $\overline{9}$ $\overline{11}$ $\overline{5}$ $\overline{3}$ $\overline{2}$ $\overline{3}$ $\overline{7}$ $\overline{7}$

Mom, what does that last word in the answer mean?

It's a small valley.

25

16 EYE CATCHERS

One letter of the alphabet is missing in each grid.
Write the missing letter in the numbered spaces below.
Then read across to find a place where rabbits live.

1

A	M	L	K	J
N	B	Z	Y	I
O	W	C	X	G
P	V	U	D	F
Q	R	S	T	E

4

A	K	L	U	V
B	J	M	T	W
D	I	N	S	X
E	H	O	R	Y
F	G	P	Q	Z

2

A	B	C	D	E
F	G	H	I	J
K	L	M	N	O
P	Q	R	S	T
V	W	X	Y	Z

5

A	B	C	D	E
L	M	N	O	P
F	G	I	J	K
Q	R	S	T	U
V	W	X	Y	Z

3

E	D	C	B	A
F	G	H	I	J
O	N	M	L	K
P	Q	R	S	U
Z	Y	X	W	V

___ ___ ___ ___ ___
 1   2   3   4   5

Hey, that's where we live!

26

FARM FUMBLERS

Can you say each of these tongue twisters three times fast?

Pigsley Is Giggly

Henley Had Hardly Any Honey

Grace Greases Geese In Greece

Dumb Duck Trick

Cows Count Crow Crowds

Forty-Five Farm Fir Trees

Cows count scow crooz . . .

AND NOW FOR
THE FARM FUMBLER FINALE
(GOOD LUCK!)

**Six Sick Chickens Checked
Six Chick's Sticks**

I REMEMBER MAMA

Curly the calf is looking for his mother. Help him find her by crossing off the cows that don't match what he's saying.

WORK FORCE

18

Follow the cross-out directions for the letters in the grid. Then write the LEFTOVER letters on the lines below. Go from left to right and top to bottom to find the name of a hard-working dog that herds sheep.

Cross out:

3 A's
4 F's
5 G's
4 H's
2 J's
3 K's
2 M's
5 N's
2 P's
2 Q's
3 S's
2 T's
2 U's
2 V's
3 W's

F	B	F	M	M	O	A
F	F	R	P	P	A	A
D	V	V	T	T	Q	E
U	U	W	R	C	Q	J
H	O	W	W	S	L	J
H	N	L	N	S	K	K
H	N	N	N	S	I	K
H	E	G	G	G	G	G

Answer: __ __ __ __ __ __ __ __ __ __ __ __

Arf

Arf

29

19 GROOMING TOOLS

The items below are used for grooming a horse. Put each word into the one spot in the grid where it will fit. Use the letters that are already written in the grid to place each word.

BRUSH

BUCKET

CLOTH

HOSE

MITT

SHAMPOO

SPONGE

TOWEL

WHAT IS IT?

Color in every shape that has a W in it to reveal something that comes in handy for a hay ride.

COLOR THAT COW

A game for two. You'll need dice and something to draw with.

Pick a cow and roll to see who goes first. Each player rolls the dice once for each turn. Color the part of your cow that matches the number of your roll. If that part is already colored, do nothing — end of turn. If you roll a 2 or 12, color any part you want! The first player to color in his/her whole cow wins.

PLAYER 1 NAME:

_____

PLAYER 2 NAME:

_____

MOVE IT AGAIN

Move the letters listed below to the same numbered spaces at the bottom of the page to find the second line of a nursery rhyme. For example, A gets moved to spaces 2 and 15.

LETTERS:

A = 2, 15
C = 10
D = 13, 17
E = 1, 8, 20
G = 6
H = 7, 19
I = 4

Just fill in these letters below.

N = 5, 16
R = 9, 12
S = 14
T = 3
U = 11
W = 18
Y = 21

NURSERY RHYME'S SECOND LINE:

__ __ __ __ __ __   __ __ __
1 2 3 4 5 6   7 8 9

__ __ __ __ __   __ __ __
10 11 12 13 14   15 16 17

__ __ __ __
18 19 20 21

Do you know this nursery rhyme?

MORNING CHORES

Fun Stuff to Move You Along

DIFFICULTY RATING:
2 HAY BALES

KIDDING AROUND

On each line there is a 5-letter word in COLUMN A and a 4-letter word in COLUMN B. The letters in both words are the same except for ONE EXTRA letter. Put that extra letter on the blank space on each line. Then read down to find the name of a breed of goat. The first one has been done for you to get you started.

COLUMN A	EXTRA LETTER	COLUMN B
LATCH	L	CHAT
CHAIN	___	CHIN
MOTOR	___	ROOT
SWEAT	___	WEST
SWING	___	WIGS
CLEAR	___	REAL
CHEAP	___	CAPE
SHADE	___	SHED

Now do the same thing again to find another breed of goat:

COLUMN A	EXTRA LETTER	COLUMN B
CRANE	___	RACE
UPSET	___	PEST
BRING	___	GRIN
ONION	___	NOON
AWAKE	___	WEAK
OPENS	___	POSE

BARN PAINTING

Henley and Pigsley had a little fun while painting the barn—they made a maze on one side! Can you find a painted path from START to END?

START

END!

BREED ALL ABOUT IT

Follow the cross-out directions for the letters in the grid. Then write the LEFTOVER letters on the blank spaces below. Go from left to right and top to bottom to find the name of a breed of cattle that is from the British Isles (England, Scotland, and Ireland).

CROSS OUT these letters every time you find them in the grid:

- Any letters that come after V in the alphabet

- Any letters that come before D in the alphabet

- The 9th letter of the alphabet

- The 10th letter of the alphabet

- The 16th letter of the alphabet

- The 17th letter of the alphabet

H	Z	A	C	X	Z
B	Z	X	J	E	B
W	Q	R	P	A	W
X	B	Z	J	Z	E
P	F	A	O	I	W
B	I	P	Y	R	W
W	Y	D	C	Y	Y

Here's a copy of the alphabet to help you:

A B C D E F G H I J K L M N O P Q R S T U V W X Y Z

Answer: __ __ __ __ __ __ __ __

Who is that handsome fellow?!!

MIRROR
MIRROR

Take a solving break! Hold this page up to a mirror to find three jokes and their answers.

WHAT DO YOU CALL A COW THAT EATS THE GRASS IN YOUR YARD?

A LAWN MOO-ER.

WHY DID THE HEN RUN AWAY?

SHE WAS TIRED OF BEING COOPED UP.

WHAT DO YOU CALL THE BOSS OF THE DAIRY?

THE BIG CHEESE.

IN

OUT

BOSS(Y)

WHAT A MESS!

Pigsley has been cleaning the barn. Can you find 10 things that are different between the BEFORE picture on this page and the AFTER picture on the next page?

BEFORE

SEE C'S

Crate starts with the letter C. Can you circle 9 other things in this picture that start with C?

GROUPIES

This word list contains 10 special words for groups of animals. Look across and down, both forward and backward, for each animal group and circle it when you find it.

DRIFT is circled and crossed off the word list to get you going. (The names of the animals are not in the grid.)

DRIFT (of swine)
DROVE (of cattle)
FLOCK (of sheep)
GAGGLE (of geese)
KINDLE (of kittens)
NEST (of pheasants)
PACE (of donkeys)
PACK (of hounds)
PEEP (of chickens)
YOKE (of oxen)

D	R	I	F	T	Z
R	L	H	L	M	Q
O	Z	V	O	E	G
V	P	A	C	K	A
E	A	T	K	O	G
M	C	S	X	Y	G
P	E	E	P	R	L
K	I	N	D	L	E

We're a peep! What are you?

ASLEEP.

43

BLANK VERSE

Can you finish writing the poems on these two pages? Each poem is missing three words. Pick words that rhyme with the CAPITALIZED words from the list next to the poem and write your answers in the blank spaces.

Pick from these words:

QUACK

CLUCK

HEE HAW

WHINNIE

TWEET

COO

AT THE MIXED-UP FARM . . .

The cow says honk
and the goose says MOO.
The dove says neigh
and the horse says _____.

The crow says oink
and the pig says CAW.
The donkey says snort
and the bull says _____.

The bird says croak
and the frog says _____.
While Farmer Brown wonders,
"What did they EAT?"

IF

If a pig could jig
and a cow could plow,
then a chick might kick
and a SOW might _____.

If a sheep could weep
and a crow could mow,
then a COLT might _____.
and a doe might throw.

If a bull could pull
and a DEER could _____,
then that donkey might conk me,
so I'm out of here!

Pick from these words:

BOLT

CHEER

JOG

BOW

FLOAT

PLUCK

Doink

DOTS THE WAY

An animal you wouldn't normally see on a farm has shown up at the barn dance. Connect the dots to find out who it is.

scritch scratch

twang

START

46

CHICKEN FEED

Change each letter below to the one that comes just BEFORE it in the alphabet.

Write each new letter on the line above the original letter. When you're done you'll learn something about chickens.

Here is a copy of the alphabet to guide you:

A B C D E F G H I J K L M N O P Q R S T U V W X Y Z

‾ ‾ ‾ ‾ ‾ ‾ ‾ ‾   ‾ ‾ ‾ ‾   ‾ ‾   ‾ ‾ ‾
D I J D L F O T   M J L F   U P   F B U

‾ ‾ ‾ ‾ ‾ ‾ ‾   ‾ ‾ ‾ ‾   ‾ ‾
D S B D L F E   D P S O   P S

‾   ‾ ‾ ‾   ‾ ‾   ‾ ‾ ‾ ‾ ‾ ‾
B   N J Y   P G   H S B J O T

‾ ‾ ‾ ‾ ‾ ‾   ‾ ‾ ‾ ‾ ‾ ‾ ‾:
D B M M F E   T D S B U D I.

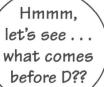

Hmmm, let's see . . . what comes before D??

Look! Here comes the answer!!

‾ ‾ ‾ ‾ ‾!
Z V N N Z!

47

GAME

FENCE ME IN

A FUN GAME FOR TWO

Take turns. On each turn, draw one line (either straight across or straight down) between two dots that are right next to each other. When you draw a line that finishes fencing in a cow, write your initial on that cow's sign. The player who fences in the most cows wins.

GAME 1   **GAME 2**

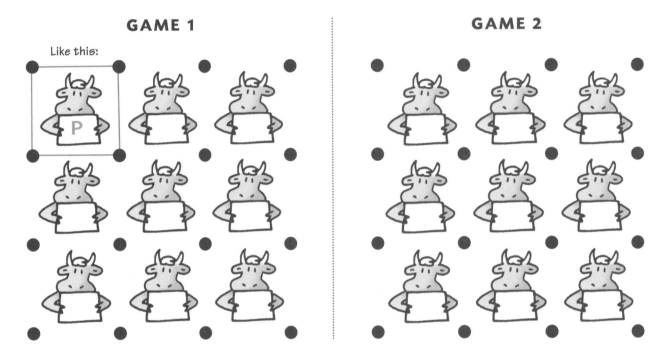

Like this:

GAME 3: Try a bigger one, this time with horses

GAME 4

GAME 5: The Grand Championship!

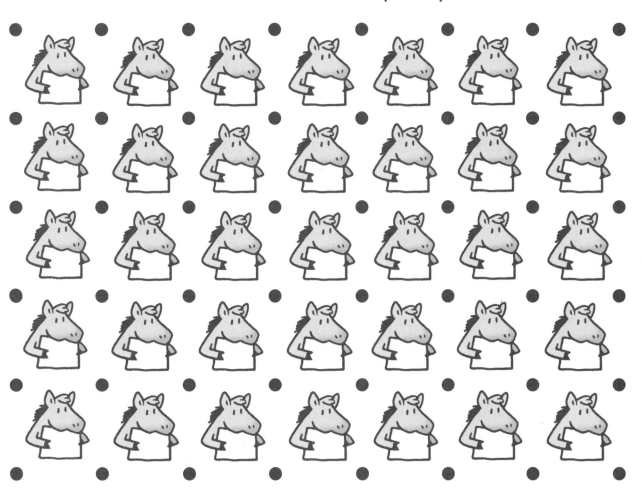

To play again, create a new field of dots on a separate piece of paper.

31 FARM FUNNIES

Pigsley and Henley have mixed up all these jokes and their answers. Can you match them up? Write the numbers of the correct joke answers in the spaces after each letter.

A: ___
Pigsley writes with a . . .

B: ___
Henley's brain is a . . .

C: ___
The ponies acted in the . . .

D: ___
The quacker paid her . . .

E: ___
When honking animals run into each other, it's called . . .

1. HORSE PLAY

2. CHICKEN NOODLE

3. PIG PEN

4. GOOSE BUMPS

5. DUCK BILL

Jokes

HAVE A BALL

Write down EVERY OTHER letter as you go around the baseball (you'll have to go around twice). The letters will spell out the answer to this joke:

Why did the farmers call their baseball team The Scrambled Eggs?

START HERE

T S H G E O Y T A B L E W A A T Y

Catch it, Mom!

Because T __ __ __ __ __ __ __ __ __

__ __ __ __ __ __ __ !

51

ANIMAL SOUNDS

CACKLE

Find 14 animal sounds in the grid. Look across, down, and diagonally (on a slant), both forward and backward for each sound and circle it when you find it. BAA is circled and crossed off the word list to get you started.

~~BAA~~
CACKLE
CAW
CROAK
GOBBLE
HEE HAW
MEOW
MOO
NEIGH
OINK
PEEP
QUACK
TWEET
WOOF

```
X  G  O  B  B  L  E
H  F  O  O  W  Z  L
G  E  P  O  I  N  K
I  Y  E  M  Q  T  C
E  M  E  H  U  E  A
N  Z  P  B  A  E  C
H  L  W  A  C  W  R
C  R  O  A  K  T  Q
```

Gobble gobble.

GOBBLE GOBBLE

ROPING CATTLE

These cattle have been practicing their lassoing. Can you figure out who has roped which post? Write the letters in the blanks.

1. ___

2. ___

3. ___

4. ___

A

B

C

D

53

WHERE, OH WHERE?

Follow the directions to find seven letters in the grid. After you find a letter be sure to write it in the blank space on each line. Then read down to find the answer to this riddle:

What state has the most cows?

FIND THE LETTER:

That is above Q and between T and P ____

That is above D and next to C ____

That is between P and G and Q and N ____

That is below G and above I ____

That is above Z and below S ____

That is below N and next to G ____

That is next to J and below Z ____

B	E	C	O
T	M	P	D
S	Q	O	N
O	F	G	R
Z	L	Y	H
K	J	I	A

FARM MATCH

Only one of these farm scenes is exactly the same as the one in the box. Circle the one that matches.

OUCH!

Put the 10 words below into the grid in order from A to J.
Then write the circled letters into the blank spaces below.
Go from top to bottom and you will find the answer to this riddle:

**What does a male cow get
when he has a pain in his tummy?**

ELVES

ITCHY

AWAKE

GAMES

CLOUD

JOKER

DOLLS

FERRY

BREAD

HATCH

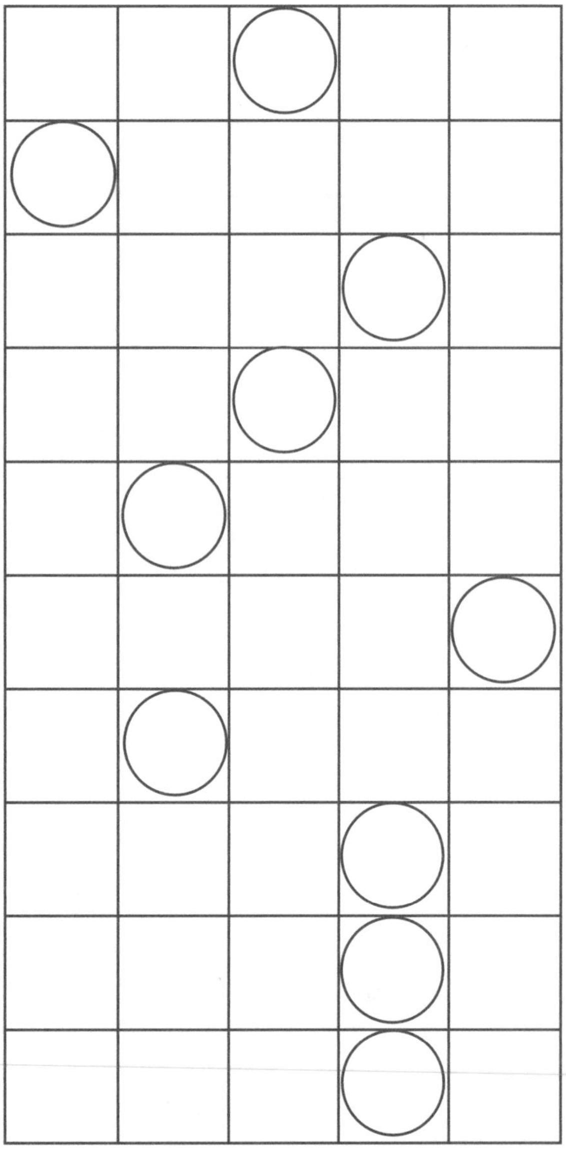

Riddle answer: __ __   __ __ __ __   __ __ __

HIDDEN ANIMALS

The animals in the box are also hidden in the sentences below. To find them, look at the letters at the end of one word and join them to the beginning of the next word. (One animal is hidden among three words.) Underline each animal you find and cross it off the list like we did for KIT.

DOE	**DOG**	**EWE**	**GOAT**
~~KIT~~	**LAMB**	**MARE**	**PIG**

LET'S <u>SKI</u> <u>TO</u>DAY.

THIS IS THE HARP I GOT.

WE PLAY BINGO AT TEN O'CLOCK.

HE CAN DO EVERYTHING.

DON'T SLAM BLUE DOORS.

WHAT DO GIRLS LIKE?

SHE WENT AWAY.

MAMA READS BOOKS.

WHEEE!

She's so smart!

HENNY PENNY

PIG PEN . . . & PENCIL

You can draw Pigsley!
Get yourself a pen and a pencil. Then just
follow these easy step-by-step instructions.

1

Using your pencil, lightly sketch an oval and a circle

Overlap them a bit

Make the circle (the body) a bit wider than the oval (the head)

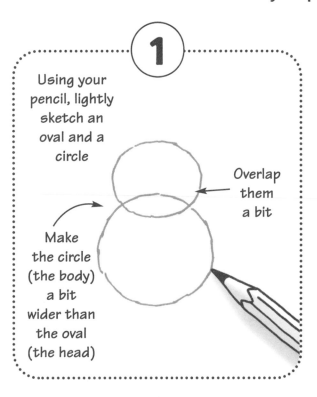

2

Draw an oval for the nose

Add two triangles for the ears

Put the nose slightly below the center of the head

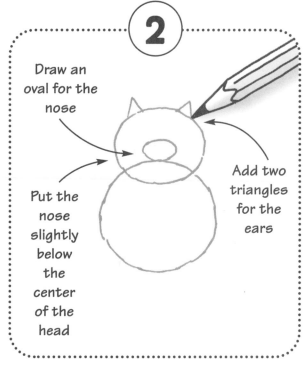

3

Sketch in legs and arms

Make them a little wider where they meet the body

4

ADD . . .

Two dots for the eyes

Two nostrils in the nose

A little, squiggly tail

And don't forget Pigsley's belly button!

PLACES ON THE FARM

The words on this list are places that can be found on a farm.
Put each word into the grid in the one spot where it fits.
Use the letters that are already in place to guide you.

4-Letter Words

BARN
COOP
NEST
POND
SHED
SILO

5-Letter Words

FIELD
HOUSE
STALL

6-Letter Words

MEADOW
STABLE

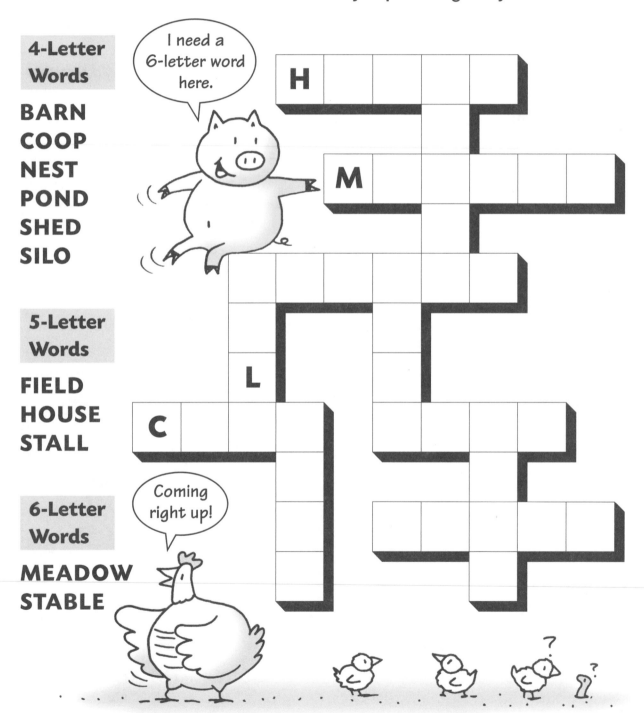

I need a 6-letter word here.

Coming right up!

60

FIELD WORK

Clever Challenges to Keep You Busy

DIFFICULTY RATING:
3 HAY BALES

CALENDAR FUN

HMMM

Put one letter into the blank space on each line to name a day of the week or a month of the year. Then read down the starred column to answer this riddle:

What do cows like to watch on Saturday night?

★

AUGUS __

MARC __

W __ DNESDAY

__ AY

M __ NDAY

OCT __ BER

NO __ EMBER

APR __ L

TU __ SDAY

__ UNDAY

Munch munch

FIELD TRIP

Henley and Pigsley are in something.
Connect the dots to find out what it is.

HORSE PLAY

Unscramble the words to make real words.
Write them on the lines. Then read everything
to find three horse riddles and their answers.

HYW SI A SHROE A DBA CRENAD?

_____

TI SAH WOT LTFE ETEF.

_____

HWY OD SRHOES VAHE DAB NERSMAN?

_____

YHET PLESE THIW EIRTH HOESS NO.

_____

OHW OD SHORES AYS ELOHL?

_____

AYH TEREH!

_____

FARMER BAAAB

Only two of these sheep farmers are exactly the same.
Can you figure out which two?

HOW CORNY

There's only one way through this
ear of corn from START to END.
Can you find it?

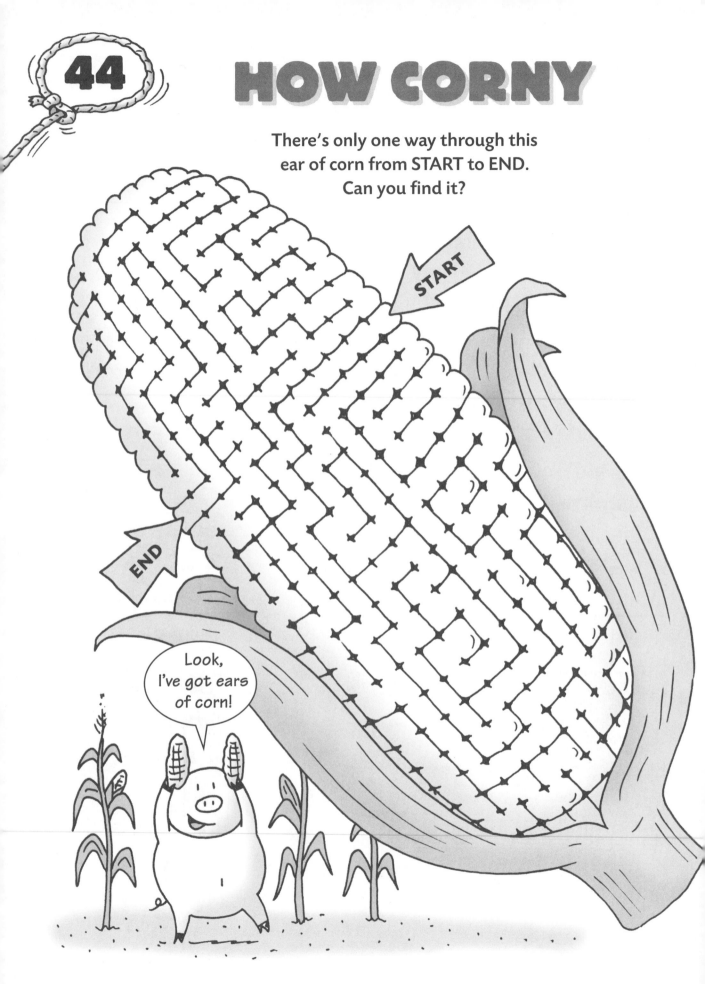

BEAST OF BURDEN

Write the answer to each clue in the grid going either ACROSS or DOWN. Then fill in the numbered spaces at the bottom of the page with the letters found in the matching numbered squares. Read across to find a hard-working farm animal that is related to the horse.

ACROSS

1. Quacking animal
3. The number before ten
4. Vegetable that can make you cry
5. Finishes (rhymes with SENDS)
6. 365 days = one ___

DOWN

2. Is very sure of (rhymes with SNOWS)
3. Type of goat (rhymes with DANNY)

I know 3-Down!

And I know 1-Across!

Answer: ___ ___ ___ ___ ___ ___
        1   4   3   2   5   6

46 BEEF IT UP

Angus cattle are black or red cows that take very good care of their calves. All the words in this list are spelled with the letters in ANGUS CATTLE. Put each word into the grid. Start with the letters that are already in place and you will fill up the grid quickly.

3-Letter Words

GAS
NUT
SET
USE

4-Letter Words

CAST
EATS
GLUE
LEGS
SALT

6-Letter Words

GLANCE
LATEST
STATUE
TALENT
UNCLES

5-Letter Words

GUEST
LANES
STATE

NUTS! TEN GNATS!

TUT TUT, A SLUG!

All those words BOTH of you said . . .

. . . They use letters from ANGUS CATTLE!

DECODE IT

In this code, pictures stand for letters.
Using the key, can you figure out the answers to these jokes?

KEY

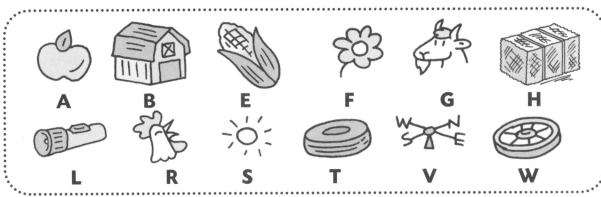

A **B** **E** **F** **G** **H**
L **R** **S** **T** **V** **W**

Who says two heads are better than one?

What do you call carrots and cabbages that insult each other?

Yer mother's a rutabaga!

How does the farmer stay so healthy?
He drinks . . .

MEMORY TEST

Henley and Pigsley are picking apples.
That's one of their favorite chores on the farm.
Study this page carefully for 60 seconds, then
turn the page and see how much you remember.

MEMORY TEST

Now, let's see how much you remember from the last page . . .

1. How many trees are in the picture?

    _____

2. How many apples are on Pigsley's tree?

    _____

3. How many apples are on Henley's tree?

    _____

4. Where are Henley's three chicks standing?

    _____

5. What is Pigsley holding?

    _____

6. How many empty bushel baskets are there on the ground?

    _____

7. How many filled bushel baskets are there on the ground?

    _____

CHEESE BOARD

Each of the six cheeses below will fit into one spot in the grid. Count the number of letters in each type of cheese and then place it in the grid that has the same number of squares. For example: a 5-letter word goes into a 5-square space.

When all the cheeses are entered, read DOWN the starred column to find a cheese that is made from sheep's milk.

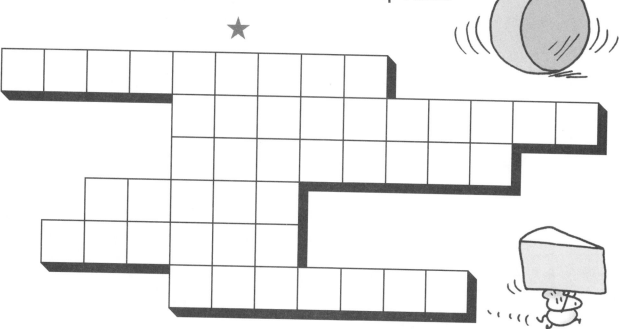

LIMBURGER

STRING

COTTAGE

MOZZARELLA

AMERICAN

CREAM

STATE DEPARTMENT

Here's a riddle for you:

Where do chickens love to vacation?

To find the answer, write one letter in each blank
to complete the name of a state in the USA.
Then read DOWN the starred column.

★

O _ IO

N _ W YORK

MAI _ E

KA _ SAS

T _ XAS

WI _ CONSIN

MIS _ OURI

V _ RMONT

D _ LAWARE

WALK THE PLANKS

These fence planks have been laid out so that Henley and her chicks can get from START to END without ever having to touch the ground. Can you figure it out?

BARREL RACING

You won't need a horse for this kind of barrel racing.

Put your pencil on the first START sign. Close your eyes and — staying between the fences — try to draw a line to barrel 1.

Stop whenever you want, open your eyes and take a look. If your pencil point hasn't stopped on the barrel, close your eyes and continue drawing from where you left off.

Count the number of times you have to OPEN your eyes. Fewer than four times is great! Try all six barrel races.

All it takes is a pencil and a pair of eyelids!

RACE 1

RACE 2

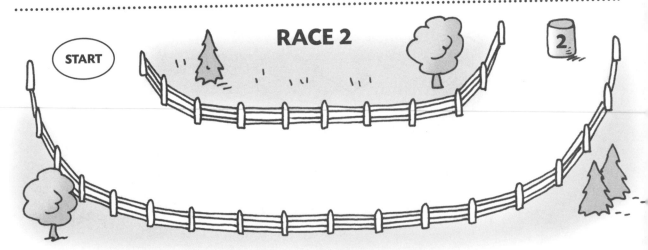

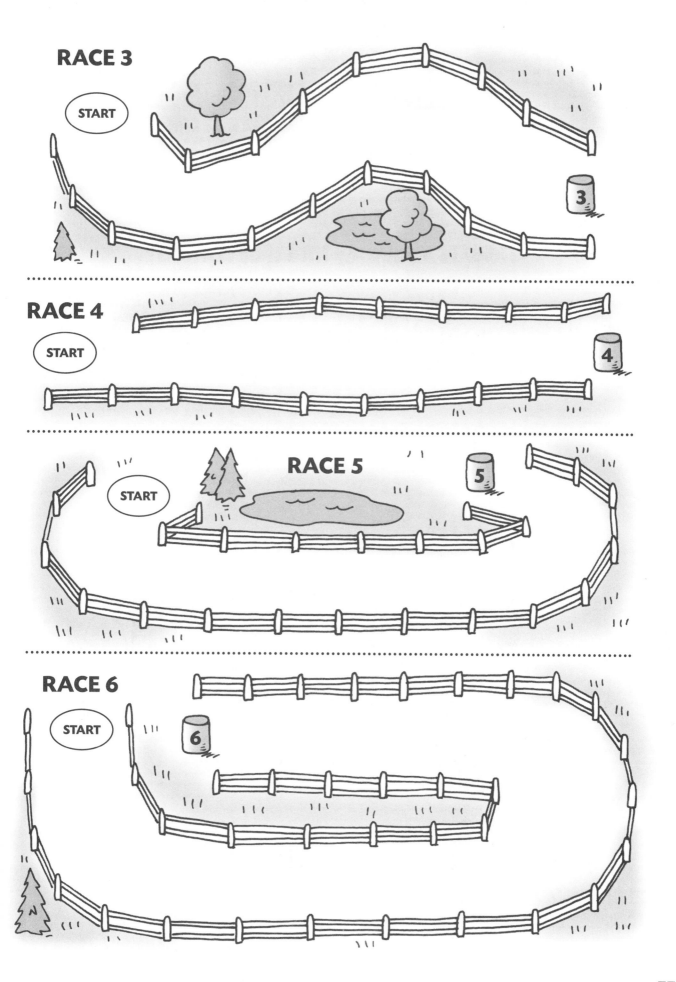

PICTURE JOKES

This kind of puzzle is called a REBUS.

The answers to these jokes have been written using pictures, letters, and words. Sometimes, you'll have to add pictures and letters together to make a word. (Two of the same thing means it's plural.)

How is a farmer like a cornfield?

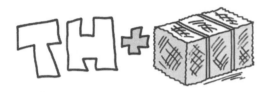

Why did the runner stop to buy lettuce?

PAIN FREE

Put each word into the grid in alphabetical order. Then read DOWN the starred column to answer this riddle:

What does a pig use for sore muscles?

★

WATERS

TUNNEL

HANDLE

REMOTE

FRIEND

SEESAW

POKING

CHOOSE

Here is a copy of the alphabet to guide you:

A B C D E F G H I J K L M N O P Q R S T U V W X Y Z

54 HORSESHOE JIGSAW

Horseshoes!

Gesundheit!

Can you match the pieces on the next page with the ones in the jigsaw puzzle below? Just write the number and then the letter of the matching piece in the blank space. The first one has been done for you.

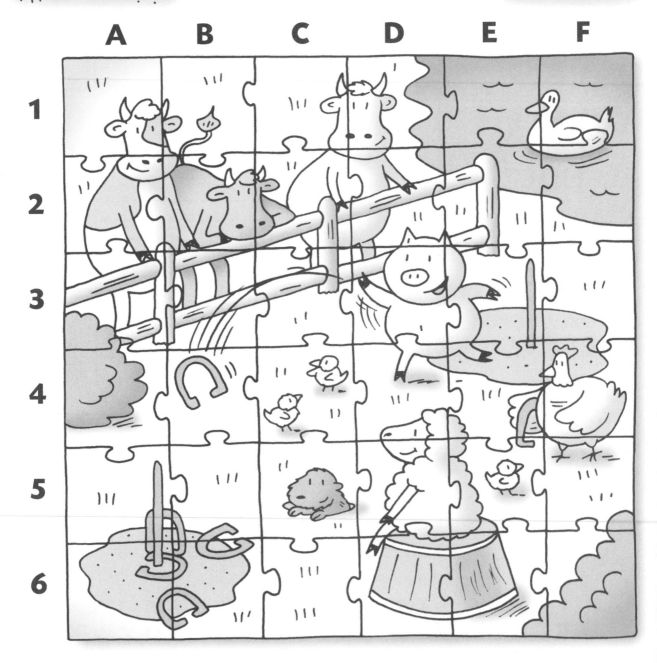

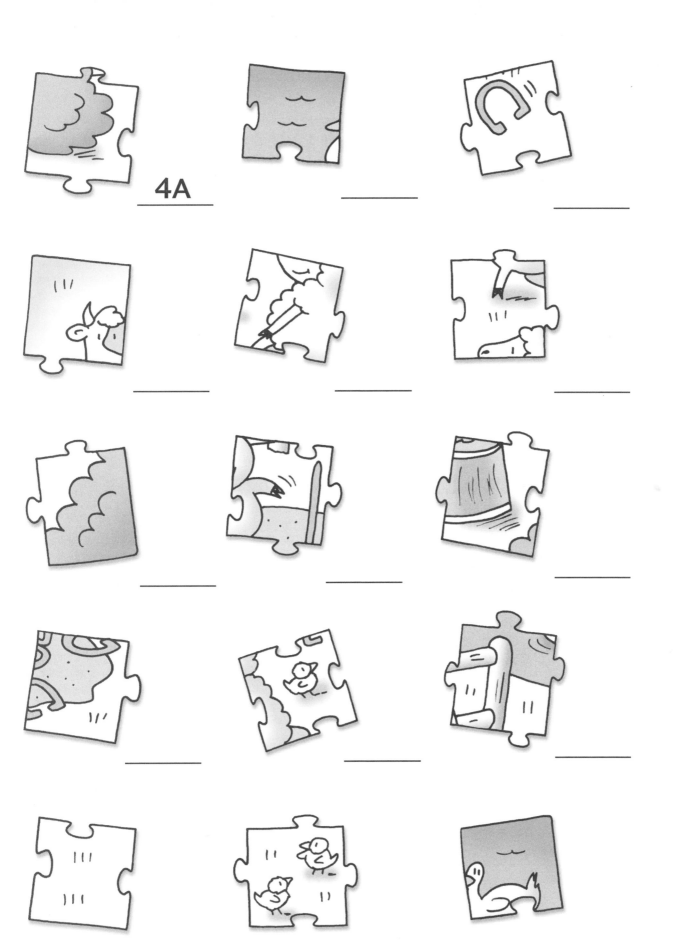

4A

81

HONKING BIRD

Write the answer to each clue in the grid going either ACROSS or DOWN. Then fill in the numbered spaces at the bottom of the page with the letters found in the matching numbered squares. Read across to find out what a male goose is called.

ACROSS

1. **Jewelry for the finger**
3. **What you smell with**
4. **The opposite of before**
5. **Animals that bark**
6. **Has a meal**

DOWN

2. **A pasture is filled with this green stuff**
3. **A doctor's helper**

Answer: ___ ___ ___ ___ ___ ___
    2   4   3   5   6   1

CRACKING UP

On each line there is a 6-letter word in COLUMN A and a 5-letter word in COLUMN B. The letters in both words are the same except for ONE EXTRA letter. Put that extra letter on the blank space on each line. Then read down to find the answer to this riddle:

What do you call a crazy chicken?

COLUMN A	EXTRA LETTER	COLUMN B
PLEASE	____	SLEEP
ARCHES	____	SHEAR
DURING	____	GRIND
BRACES	____	BEARS
ANKLES	____	LEANS
HOOVES	____	SHOVE
SPOILS	____	SLIPS
CLOSET	____	STOLE
CRADLE	____	RACED
SPROUT	____	SPORT
SEARCH	____	HEARS
SKATER	____	STARE

83

GRID DRAWING

You can draw Henley — one square at a time!
Fill in the grid on the next page by drawing exactly what you see in
each square of the grid below. Use the letters and numbers to make
sure you're drawing in the right squares.

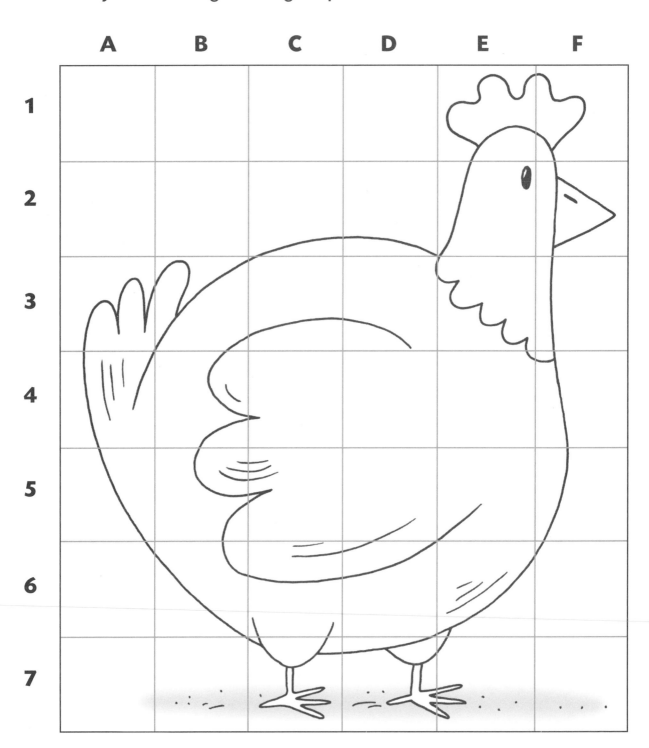

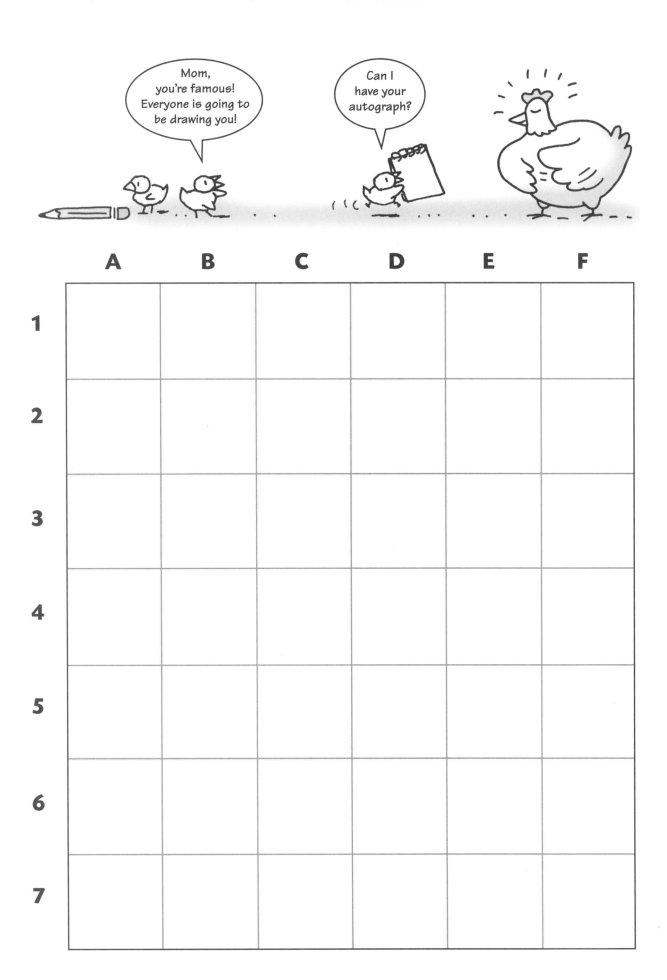

END OF THE LINE

Add one letter to the end of each group of letters to make a word that finishes the sentence. Then read DOWN to find the answer to this riddle:

What do you call an office building for pigs?

The largest state is.. **ALASK** ___

A window is made of.. **GLAS** ___

The opposite of slow is.. **FAS** ___

The number after 19 is... **TWENT** ___

The opposite of more is.. **LES** ___

The top part of a house is the.................................. **ATTI** ___

The opposite of over is... **UNDE** ___

The largest continent is... **ASI** ___

An 8-sided red traffic sign says............................... **STO** ___

When something doesn't cost anything it is...... **FRE** ___

A person who gets the gold medal is the.............. **WINNE** ___

EVENING ROUND-UP

Tough Teasers to Show How Smart You are

DIFFICULTY RATING:

4 HAY BALES

58 COWS IN CLOVER

Complete each of the joke answers by putting 2, 3, or 4 of the letters from the word CLOVER in the blank spaces.

The letters must be in the same order as they appear in CLOVER, and you can't skip letters. For example, you can use LO but not LE or VO.

Q: **How do you fit five cows into a convertible?**

A: **Two in the front, two in the back, and**

one in the G __ __ __ __ compartment.

Q: **How can you tell if there are**

four cows in your refrigerator?

A: **The door won't __ __ __ SE.**

Q: **What's worse than four cows**

in your refrigerator?

A: **FI __ __ cows in your**

refrigerator.

Q: **How can you tell if there are**

five cows in your refrigerator?

A: **There's an empty**

CON __ __ __ TIBLE parked out back.

Q: **What's worse than five cows in your refrigerator?**

A: **Five cows in your __ __ __ N.**

OPPOSITE DISTRACTION 1

Fill in the answer blanks with a word that means the **OPPOSITE** of the word on the left. The new word you make answers the clue on the right.

	ANSWER	CLUE
SUBTRACT	S _ _ _ _ L E	Horseback rider's seat
STAY	_ _ A T	Farm animal with horns
OPEN	F _ _ _ _ _	Group of sheep
OFF	P _ _ Y	Small horse
NOTHING	S T _ _ _ _	Part of a stable
FUTURE	_ _ _ _ U R E	Grazing area
COOKED	S T _ _ _ _	Bedding material for animals

That's a very clever puzzle!

Cleverest puzzle on the whole page.

Heh heh! Good one, Mom!

RHODE ISLAND RED WORDS

A Rhode Island Red is a popular breed of chicken with reddish brown feathers. All the words below are spelled using the letters in **RHODE ISLAND RED**.

Can you put each word into the grid on the next page? Start with the letters that are already in place and you will fill up the grid quickly.

3-Letter Words

EEL
RAN
SEA

4-Letter Words

DISH
EARN
HERD
LAND
NAIL
NEAR
RAIN

5-Letter Words

DRAIN
EASEL
ORDER
SNORE

6-Letter Words

HAIRDO
HANDLE
SENIOR

OH DEAR, DO I DARE?

Mom, all those words you just said — they use letters from RHODE ISLAND RED!

SICK DAZE

Cross off the words in the box using the instructions at the bottom of the page. Then read the leftover words from BOTTOM to TOP to find the answer to this riddle:

Why did the mama horse feel sick?

BARN	COLT	YELLOW	PIN
FIN	BUTTER	BAD	THANKSGIVING
GREEN	VERY	MILK	CARROT
NOSE	RED	CUCUMBER	ORANGE
CHEESE	A	HALLOWEEN	YOGURT
EYE	WIN	MOUTH	RADISH
HAD	CHRISTMAS	EASTER	STABLE
LETTUCE	BLUE	SHE	BIN

CROSS OFF:

- 4 holidays
- 5 colors
- 4 vegetables
- 4 dairy products
- 2 farm buildings
- 3 face parts
- 4 words that rhyme with TIN

LOVE LETTERS

Each animal mailed out one of these Valentine's Day cards. Can you figure out who mailed out which by reading the sayings and thinking "punny"? Write the number of the card above the animal that sent it.

A. ___

B. ___

C. ___

D. ___

E. ___

1

HOPPY VALENTINE'S DAY

2

will EWE be mine?

3

I'm Purrfect for you!

4

I'LL QUACK UP WITHOUT YOU

5

I'm not KIDDING, I like YOU.

MISSING IN ACTION

Some of the veggies that farmers grow are listed here, but each one is missing a three-letter word. Take one word from the box, put it into the blank spaces on each line, and name the veggie. Cross off each word as you use it because it will be used one time only.

ASH	BAG	BEE
LET	LOW	PEP	PIN
RAG	ROT	WEE

CAB __ __ __ E

S __ __ __ T POTATO

CAULIF __ __ __ ER

ASPA __ __ __ US

SQU __ __ __

__ __ __ T

__ __ __ PER

CAR __ __ __

__ __ __ TUCE

S __ __ __ ACH

Now do the same thing to name a fruit on each line.
Use the three-letter words from the box below.

APE ATE CAN

COT EAR HER ONE

RAN RAW TAN

W__ __ __RMELON

APRI__ __ __

H__ __ __YDEW

P__ __ __

ST__ __ __BERRY

O__ __ __GE

__ __ __TALOUPE

GR__ __ __

__ __ __GERINE

C__ __ __RY

ROAD HOG

You "auto" have a lot of fun with this puzzle. Fourteen car parts are hidden in the grid. Look across, down, and diagonally (on a slant) both forward and backward for each term.

Circle each car part when you find it. Then put the LEFTOVER letters into the blank spaces below. Go from left to right and top to bottom to find the answer to this riddle:

Where does a hog keep its car?

AERIAL
AIR BAG
DOOR
ENGINE
FAN
FENDER
HEATER
HORN
PEDAL
RADIO
SEAT BELT
TANK
TIRE
TRUNK

P	E	D	A	L	I	R	S
H	N	R	E	T	A	E	H
O	T	H	I	D	A	N	E
R	P	O	I	T	R	G	G
N	R	O	B	R	O	I	A
K	A	E	I	U	O	N	B
N	L	F	E	N	D	E	R
T	A	N	K	K	G	L	I
O	T	L	A	I	R	E	A

Riddle answer: __ __ __ __ __ __ __ __ __ __ __ __ __ __ __ __

DITCH DIGGERS

Pigsley and Henley have dug an irrigation ditch to get water to their crops. Can you find the TWO routes that go from the pond to the field?

START

START

FIELD

END

FAMILY TIES

Add one letter to the start of each group of letters to make a word that finishes the sentence. Then read DOWN to find a term that describes someone who fusses over people the way a chicken fusses over its young.

A field used for grazing is a............................... __EADOW

A body of water like the Pacific is an............ __CEAN

A farm vehicle with large tires is a................ __RACTOR

The "Aloha State" is.. __AWAII

To clean a chalkboard you use an.................... __RASER

A male chicken is a.. __OOSTER

A large bird of prey with sharp claws is a.... __AWK

The planet you live on is................................... __ARTH

The opposite of ALL is...................................... __OTHING

Clank clank

Mom, you REALLY need to try this puzzle!

IT'S ABOUT TIME

Fifteen words related to time are hidden in the grid. Look across, down, and diagonally (on a slant) both forward and backward for each term. Circle it when you find it.

After you have found and circled all the words put the LEFTOVER letters into the blank spaces below. Keep the letters in order from left to right and top to bottom and you will find the answer to this riddle:

What horse never goes out during the day?

DAWN		M	O	M	E	N	T	S	A
DAY		I	O	E	D	A	C	E	D
DECADE		N	N	R	I	N	W	A	D
ERA		U	G	H	N	A	P	S	M
EVE		T	T	M	Y	I	A	O	R
HOUR		E	W	E	E	K	N	N	E
MINUTE		D	A	Y	V	T	R	G	T
MOMENT		R	U	O	H	E	R	A	E
MONTH
MORNING
SEASON
SPAN
TERM
WEEK
YEAR

Riddle answer: __ __ __ __ __ __ __ __ __ __

68 PICTURE CROSSWORD

Below are 17 things you might find around a farm. Write the names of the pictures in the grid on the next page. We filled in 14-Across to get you started.

ACROSS

1-ACROSS

3-ACROSS

6-ACROSS

8-ACROSS

10-ACROSS

12-ACROSS

14-ACROSS

15-ACROSS

16-ACROSS

DOWN

2-DOWN

5-DOWN

4-DOWN

7-DOWN

9-DOWN

11-DOWN

12-DOWN

13-DOWN

FIVE BARNS

Can you find a route that visits all five barns exactly once?
You can't go over the same section of road twice.
There's only one way to do it.

START

END

ANNIE'S GRAM

Annie's Gram (Grandma) likes to write sentences for Annie. These sentences always contain two words that are anagrams of each other. This means that they use the same letters to spell two different words, like NOW and WON.

Can you find the two three-letter anagrams in each sentence below? Underline the words when you find them.

OUR CAT MIGHT ACT FUNNY.

HE WROTE AN ODE TO HIS DOE.

THE OWL SLEEPS ON A LOW BEAM IN THE BARN.

THAT EWE IS WEE.

THE RAM CAN MAR LOTS OF THINGS.

I DREW A PICTURE OF A RAT IN MY ART CLASS.

I'VE GOT A CODE

Using these two codes, can you
decode Pigsley and Henley's jokes?

THE SWITCH CODE

To decode a message using this code, all you have to
do is switch lines using the decoder below. For example,
A is written as the letter below it — Z — and an X is
written as the letter above it — B. Just switch lines!

A	B	C	D	E	F	G	H	I	J	K	L	M
Z	X	Y	W	V	U	T	S	R	Q	P	O	N

Henley and Pigsley have used the SWITCH CODE for this joke:

Decode this joke using the NUMBER CODE instructions below.

THE NUMBER CODE

In this code, every letter is written using two numbers.

For example, G is written as 27. That's because G is the letter where 2 and 7 cross. (The left number in the chart is always written first.)

Every letter is a different two number combination, except for Y and Z. They're both 50, but you'll be able to figure out which letter 50 stands for by the way it's used in the word.

	6	7	8	9	0
1	A	B	C	D	E
2	F	G	H	I	J
3	K	L	M	N	O
4	P	Q	R	S	T
5	U	V	W	X	YZ

MIDDLE OF THE ROAD

Fill in the middle space on each line to name a word that fits the clue. Then read DOWN the starred column to find the answer to this riddle:

 Oh boy, riddles!

What amusement park ride do calves like?

 Woo hoo! Let's do 'em!

★

Thin piece of wood used to light fires............ MA ___ CH

A person who seats you in a theater............ US ___ ER

Crawl like a baby................................. CR ___ EP

Breakfast meat that goes with eggs............ BA ___ ON

A tool used for sweeping........................ BR ___ OM

A cloth used for drying......................... TO ___ EL

The number before four......................... TH ___ EE

The color of dirt............................... BR ___ WN

Small rodent with a long tail.................. MO ___ SE

A rope used by a cowboy........................ LA ___ SO

Rest time during the night..................... SL ___ EP

Foolish.. SI ___ LY

Now do the same thing to find the answer to this riddle:

What did the pony say when he had a sore throat?

★

Moves in water..	SW __ MS
The color of a crow..	BL __ CK
Ten-cent coins..	DI __ ES
A device used for weighing	SC __ LE
Food that goes with peanut butter......................	JE __ LY
Very fast..	QU __ CK
Part of a flower..	PE __ AL
Go inside...	EN __ ER
Hi there!..	HE __ LO
The wife of a king..	QU __ EN
Leftover stuff in a fireplace...................................	AS __ ES
Funny person at a circus...	CL __ WN
Get up from a chair..	ST __ ND
The month after February.......................................	MA __ CH
Glue..	PA __ TE
Not sour...	SW __ ET

TRUE/FALSE

Read each sentence below and decide if it's TRUE or FALSE. If it's TRUE, circle the letter in the TRUE column; if it's FALSE, circle the letter in the FALSE column. When you're finished, read the circled letters from 1 to 7 to find the two-word answer to this riddle:

What do you call two pigs who live together?

	TRUE	FALSE
1. **A bantam is a miniature chicken**..................................	P	R
2. **A buck is a female goat**...	A	E
3. **A lamb is a sheep that is less than one year old**.....	N	M
4. **A draft horse is used for farm work**........................	P	G
5. **Free-range chickens roam about to find food**.........	A	I
6. **Goats and sheep never have to be sheared**..............	B	L
7. **Angus and Hereford are breeds of sheep**..................	R	S

Aah! Nothing like a nice, cool mud bath on a hot day.

Except maybe a nice, hot mud bath on a cold day.

OPPOSITE DISTRACTION 2

Fill in the answer blanks with a word that means the OPPOSITE of the word on the left. The new word you make answers the clue on the right.

	ANSWER	CLUE
ENEMY	_ _ _ O M I N O	A horse color
DRY	_ _ _ H E R	A male sheep
LOSE	S _ _ _ E	Hogs and pigs
SHORT	S _ _ _ _ I O N	Male horse
HE	_ _ _ A R	Remove wool from a sheep
HEALTHY	B _ _ _ Y	Type of goat
OUT	_ _ C U B A T O R	Mechanical device for hatching eggs

Hmm . . . I think I figured out the second one, but I'm not quite sure.

The answer sounds like the forecast on the news — if it's going to be cold and rainy, for example.

But it's spelled differently, right Mom?

109

TRACTOR RACE

Who can race their tractor back to the barn first?
A game for 1 to 4 players using 3 coins instead of dice.

Find a small item (button, paper clip, etc.) to be your playing piece.
Shake 3 coins (any type of coins) in your hands and drop them.
Move your playing piece the number of spaces shown on the chart.
Take turns. First player to reach the barn, wins!

If you're alone, you can play with us.

MOVING CHART

1 TAIL (2 HEADS) — MOVE 1 SPACE
2 TAILS (1 HEAD) — MOVE 2 SPACES
3 TAILS (0 HEADS) — MOVE 3 SPACES
0 TAILS (3 HEADS) — MOVE 4 SPACES

Just put extra playing pieces down and move for us.

START

GO BACK TO START

MAKE A TRACTOR "VROOM VROOM" SOUND

SLIP AHEAD ONE

SWITCH PLACES WITH ANY PLAYER

YOU'RE STUCK IN MUD – LOSE ONE TURN

RACE FORWARD 3 SPACES

TRACTOR STALLS – GO BACK 2 SPACES

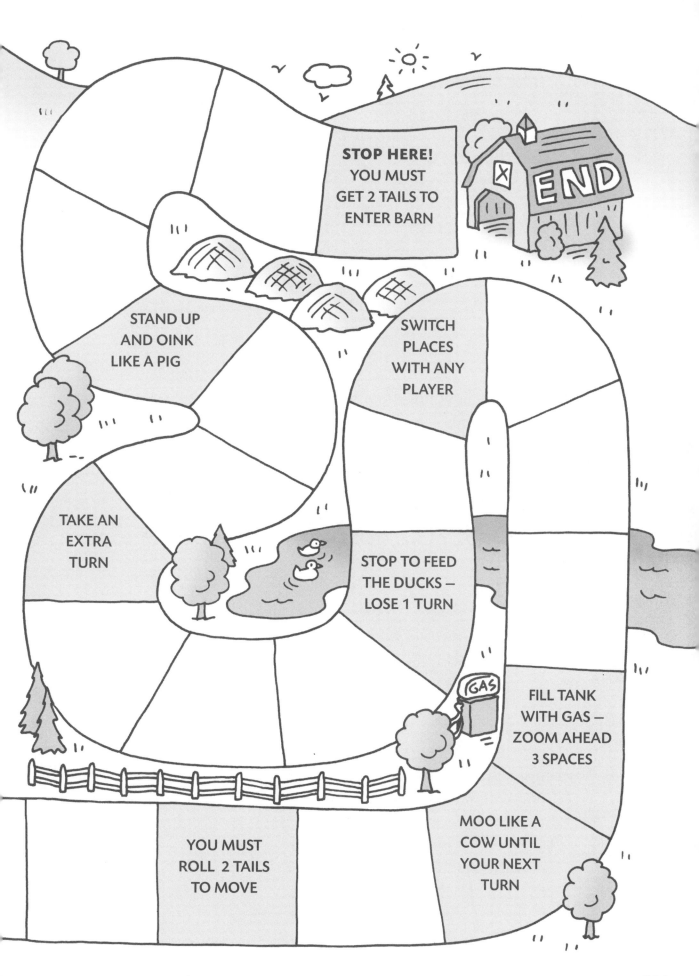

STOP HERE!
YOU MUST
GET 2 TAILS TO
ENTER BARN

END

STAND UP
AND OINK
LIKE A PIG

SWITCH
PLACES
WITH ANY
PLAYER

TAKE AN
EXTRA
TURN

STOP TO FEED
THE DUCKS —
LOSE 1 TURN

GAS

FILL TANK
WITH GAS —
ZOOM AHEAD
3 SPACES

YOU MUST
ROLL 2 TAILS
TO MOVE

MOO LIKE A
COW UNTIL
YOUR NEXT
TURN

75 WHO IS IT?

Want to know who we think is the best puzzle solver ever?

Carefully follow these 5 steps to find out!

1. Pick a number: 1, 2, 3, 4, or 5 ⟶ write it here: ___

2. Add 200 to it ⟶ + 2 0 0

TOTAL = ___ ___ ___

3. What is the first letter of your first name?
Find it here and add the number next to it:

> A, B, C, D, E, F, or G — add 5
> H, I, J, K, L, or M — add 6
> N, O, P, Q, R, or S — add 7
> T, U, V, W, X, Y, or Z — add 8

⟶ + ___

NEW TOTAL = ___ ___ ___

4. Look at the NEW TOTAL.

If the last number is higher than 5, add 10
If the last number is exactly 5, add 8
If the last number is less than 5, add 6

⟶ + ___ ___

FINAL TOTAL = ___ ___ ___

5. Change the 3 numbers in the FINAL
TOTAL to letters using this chart:

> 1st number: 1=D 2=Y 3=R 4=S
> 2nd number: 1=O 2=A 3=E 4=I
> 3rd number: 1 to 4=T   6 to 9=U

ANSWER:

IT'S ___ ___ ___ !

BARNYARD DICTIONARY

A dictionary and word quiz in one!

On the next two pages are some words that appear in this book. Most are farm words, but a few aren't. Cover up the definitions (they're on the right) and see how many words you know without looking. Close enough counts! Put a check mark in the box next to every word you get right.

☐	**BREED**	A group of animals that have common features.
☐	**CALF**	A young cow (plural: calves).
☐	**CATTLE**	Cows, bulls, and calves.
☐	**COLT**	A young male horse.
☐	**CONVERTIBLE**	A car whose top can fold down.
☐	**COW**	Although a cow is a female, people often use cow or cows to mean both males and females. We've done the same thing in a few places in this book.
☐	**DOE**	The female of animals such as rabbits or deer.
☐	**DUCK BILL**	A duck's beak.
☐	**EWE**	An adult female sheep.
☐	**FILLY**	A young female horse.
☐	**FOAL**	A newborn horse.
☐	**GANDER**	A male goose.
☐	**GESUNDHEIT**	A word people say when someone sneezes. (Did you know it actually means "health" in German?)
☐	**GRASS HAY**	A mixture of hays used for horse food.
☐	**HORSEPLAY**	Rowdy or rough play.
☐	**HUTCH**	A small pen for rabbits.
☐	**JIG**	A lively dance common in Ireland.

☐	**KID**	A young goat.
☐	**MAR**	To damage or hurt.
☐	**MARE**	An adult female or mother horse.
☐	**MEADOW**	A grassy area where animals graze (also called a pasture).
☐	**NIGHTMARE**	A bad dream.
☐	**NOODLE**	A slang word for your brain.
☐	**ODE**	A type of poem.
☐	**OINTMENT**	A cream that is put on cuts and burns.
☐	**RAM**	An adult male sheep.
☐	**SHOAT**	A young pig.
☐	**SILO**	A farm building used for storing animal food.
☐	**SKYSCRAPER**	A very tall building.
☐	**STABLE**	A building where horses are kept.
☐	**STALL**	A small room in a stable, usually for one horse.
☐	**TUFFET**	A low seat like a stool.

How many words did you know?

Count up all the check marks, then turn the page to see how you rate ⟶

BARNYARD DICTIONARY

HOW DID YOU DO?

There are 32 words in the dictionary.
Count one point for every one you knew
without looking and see how you rate:

5   **GOOD**
10   **GREAT**
15   **FABULOUS**
20   **ABSOLUTELY AM-A-A-A-ZING!**
25   **HELLO, BRAINIAC**
30   **WE'RE BEYOND STUNNED**

**If you got them all, your name must
be Noah Webster** (he wrote dictionaries) **!**

THE ANSWERS

RISE AND SHINE

1 **EASY AS PIE**
Page 10

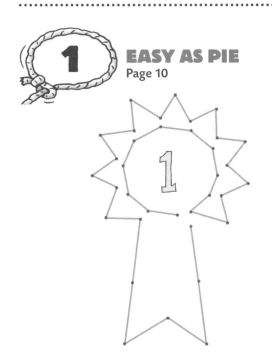

2 **DAIRY PRODUCTS**
Page 11

3 **COOP SCOOP**
Pages 12–13

4 PARENT/CHILD MATCH-UP
Page 14

ANSWER:
COW – CALF CAT – KITTEN CHICKEN – CHICK
HORSE – FOAL SHEEP – LAMB RABBIT – BUNNY

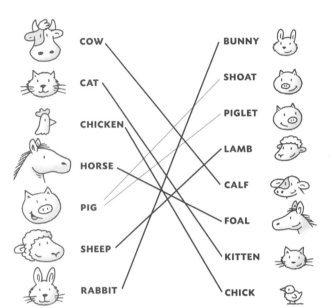

5 BABY ANIMALS
Page 15

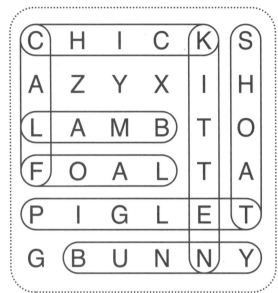

6 IN THE BARN
Page 16

7 MOVE IT
Page 17

ANSWER:

OLD MACDONALD HAD A FARM!

8 CHECK THIS OUT
Page 18

ANSWER:

WHAT DO FARM CATS EAT ON A HOT DAY?
MICE CREAM

★ WHY   ✕ WHEN   ▼ WHERE   (✓ WHAT)   ● WHO

✕ DID   ● DON'T   ★ WILL   ▼ WOULD   (✓ DO)   ■ DIDN'T   ✚ COULD

✚ BARN   ● STALL   (✓ FARM)   ★ MEADOW   ✕ STABLE   ▼ SILO

(✓ CATS)   ▼ DOGS   ■ FROGS   ✕ RABBITS   ● BUNNIES   ✚ HORSES

■ DINE   ✚ MUNCH   ● CHEW   ★ DRINK   (✓ EAT)

▼ IN   (✓ ON)   ■ OUT   ✕ WITH   ★ OVER

✚ THE   ● AN   (✓ A)   ▼ ANY   ■ SOME

● COLD   ✕ WINDY   (✓ HOT)   ★ STORMY   ▼ RAINY

(✓ DAY?)   ✚ NIGHT?   ● MORNING?   ✕ AFTERNOON?   ★ EVENING?

✕ RAT   ▼ FLEA   ● RODENT   (✓ MICE)   ★ LOCUST

★ MILK   (✓ CREAM)   ▼ YOGURT   ● CHEESE

9 HORSE FOOD
Page 19

ANSWER:
GRASS HAY

Giraffe
Rabbit
Apple
Snake
Saw

Hand
Arrow
Yo-yo

10 WHAT'S WRONG?
Page 20

1. Octagon-shaped sun
2. Wrong letter on weather vane
3. Truck in sky
4. Upside-down tree
5. Sideways barn
6. Big ice cream cone
7. Doughnut tractor tire
8. Two handles on axe
9. Cornstalk fence post
10. Square bicycle wheel

11 TWO FOR ONE
Page 21

ANSWER:

BUCK.

It's in the top grid, but not in the bottom one.

12 THREESIES
Page 22

ANSWER:
A BOX OF QUACKERS

D	Ⓐ	G	G	Ⓑ	I	I	D
D	G	Ⓞ	N	Ⓧ	I	Ⓞ	M
M	M	N	N	P	T	Ⓕ	V
V	Ⓠ	P	P	T	T	V	Ⓤ
Z	W	W	Y	Y	Y	Z	Ⓐ
Ⓒ	W	Ⓚ	L	Z	Ⓔ	J	J
J	L	L	Ⓡ	H	H	H	Ⓢ

13 ORDER! ORDER!
Page 23

14 WORM SQUIRM
Page 24

15 SING ALONG
Page 25

ANSWER:

THE FARMER IN THE DELL!

16 EYE CATCHERS
Page 26

ANSWER:

HUTCH.

17 I REMEMBER MAMA
Page 28

My mom is circled.

18 WORK FORCE
Page 29

ANSWER:
BORDER COLLIE

F	Ⓑ	F	M	M	Ⓞ	A
F	F	Ⓡ	P	P	A	A
Ⓓ	V	V	T	T	Q	Ⓔ
U	U	W	Ⓡ	Ⓒ	Q	J
H	Ⓞ	W	W	S	Ⓛ	J
H	N	Ⓛ	N	S	K	K
H	N	N	N	S	Ⓘ	K
H	Ⓔ	G	G	G	G	

19 GROOMING TOOLS
Page 30

20 WHAT IS IT?
Page 31

It's a wagon wheel!

21 MOVE IT AGAIN
Page 34

ANSWER:

EATING HER CURDS AND WHEY.

② MORNING CHORES

22 KIDDING AROUND
Page 36

ANSWERS:
LAMANCHA
and
NUBIAN

23 BARN PAINTING
Page 37

START

END!

24 BREED ALL ABOUT IT
Page 38

ANSWER:
HEREFORD

25 WHAT A MESS!
Page 40-41

1. Jar on shelf
2. Longer pulley rope
3. Hay bale behind Pigsley
4. Cloud in front of sun
5. Turkey in doorway
6. Chick on left front hay bale
7. Spills on floor
8. 2nd milk canister
9. 2nd glove on bale
10. Pitchfork handle

26 SEE C'S
Page 42

ANSWER:
CHICKEN, CUP, CANDLE, CAP, COW,
CARROTS, CORN, CRAYON, CAN

27 GROUPIES
Page 43

28 BLANK VERSE
Pages 44-45

ANSWERS:

COO, HEE HAW, TWEET
and
BOW, BOLT, CHEER

29 DOTS THE WAY
Page 46

30 CHICKEN FEED
Page 47

ANSWER:

Chickens like to eat cracked corn or a mix of grains called scratch. Yummy!

31 FARM FUNNIES
Page 50

ANSWER:

A: 3 Pigsley writes with a pig pen.
B: 2 Henley's brain is a chicken noodle.
C: 1 The ponies acted in the horse play.
D: 5 The quacker paid her duck bill.
E: 4 When honking animals run into each other, it's called goose bumps.

32 HAVE A BALL
Page 51

ANSWER:

Because
THEY ALWAYS GOT BEAT!

33 ANIMAL SOUNDS
Page 52

```
X  G  O  B  B  L  E
H  F  O  O  W  Z  L
G  E  P  O  I  N  K
I  Y  E  M  Q  T  C
E  M  E  H  U  E  A
N  Z  P  B  A  E  C
H  L  W  A  C  W  R
C  R  O  A  K  T  Q
```

34 ROPING CATTLE
Page 53

ANSWER:
1: C   2: B   3: D   4: A

35 WHERE, OH WHERE?
Page 54

ANSWER:

M O O Y O R K

36 FARM MATCH
Page 55

ANSWER:
NUMBER 3

37 OUCH!
Page 56

ANSWER:
A BULLY (BELLY) ACHE

A	W	A	K	E
B	R	E	A	D
C	L	O	U	D
D	O	L	L	S
E	L	V	E	S
F	E	R	R	Y
G	A	M	E	S
H	A	T	C	H
I	T	C	H	Y
J	O	K	E	R

39 PLACES ON THE FARM
Page 60

38 HIDDEN ANIMALS
Page 57

LET'S SKI TODAY. **KIT**

THIS IS THE HARP I GOT. **PIG**

WE PLAY BINGO AT TEN O'CLOCK. **GOAT**

HE CAN DO EVERYTHING. **DOE**

DON'T SLAM BLUE DOORS. **LAMB**

WHAT DO GIRLS LIKE? **DOG**

SHE WENT AWAY. **EWE**

MAMA READS BOOKS. **MARE**

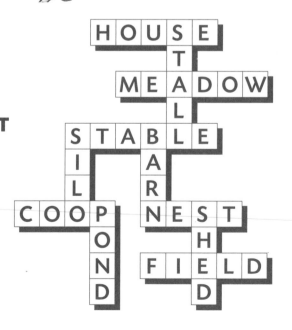

③
FIELD WORK

40 CALENDAR FUN
Page 62

ANSWER:

THE MOO-VIES.
(movies)

41 FIELD TRIP
Page 63

42 HORSE PLAY
Page 64

ANSWERS:

1. WHY IS A HORSE A BAD DANCER?
IT HAS TWO LEFT FEET.

2. WHY DO HORSES HAVE BAD MANNERS?
THEY SLEEP WITH THEIR SHOES ON.

3. HOW DO HORSES SAY HELLO?
HAY THERE!

43 FARMER BAAAB
Page 65

ANSWER:
3 and 5 are exactly the same.

44 HOW CORNY
Page 66

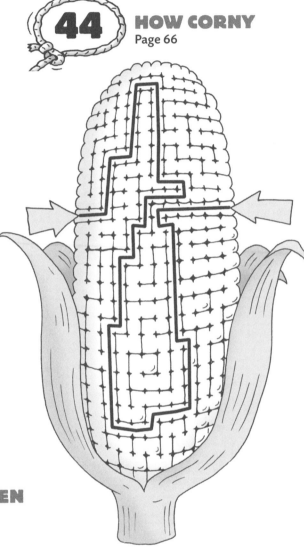

45 BEAST OF BURDEN
Page 67

ANSWER:
DONKEY

D	U	C	K			N	I	N	E
		N				A			
		O	N	I	O	N			
		W				N			
E	N	D	S			Y	E	A	R

46 BEEF IT UP
Pages 68-69

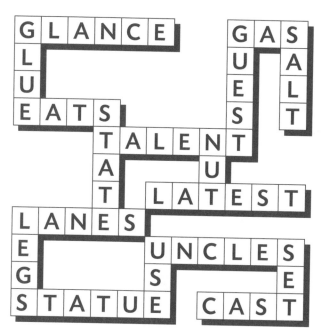

47 DECODE IT
Page 70

ANSWERS:

FRESH VEGETABLES

WELL WATER

48 MEMORY TEST
Pages 71-72

1. There are 3 trees.
2. Pigsley's tree has 3 apples.
3. Henley's tree has 5 apples.
4. The chicks aren't in the picture!
5. Pigsley is holding a bucket (or pail).
6. There are 2 empty bushel baskets.
7. There are 3 filled bushel baskets.

49 CHEESE BOARD
Page 73

ANSWER:
ROMANO

★

LIMBURGER
MOZZARELLA
AMERICAN
CREAM
STRING
COTTAGE

50 STATE DEPARTMENT
Page 74

ANSWER:
HENNESSEE
(Tennessee)

51 WALK THE PLANKS
Page 75

START

END

52 PICTURE JOKES
Page 78

ANSWERS:

TH + hay bow + TH
HAVE ears =
They both have ears.

bee + caws SHE
WANTED 2
GET A head =
Because she wanted
to get ahead (a head).

53 PAIN FREE
Page 79

ANSWER:
OINKMENT
(ointment)

★

C	H	O	O	S	E	
F	R	I	E	N	D	
H	A	N	D	L	E	
P	O	K	I	N	G	
R	E	M	O	T	E	
S	E	E	S	A	W	
T	U	N	N	E	L	
W	A	T	E	R	S	

54 HORSESHOE JIGSAW
Pages 80-81

 4A   1E    4B

 1A   5D   4D

 6F   3E   6E

 6B   5E   2E

6C   4C   1F

55 HONKING BIRD
Page 82

ANSWER:
GANDER

R	I	N	G				N	O	S	E
			R				U			
			A	F	T	E	R			
			S				S			
	D	O	G	S			E	A	T	S

133

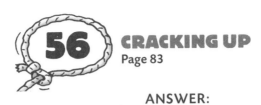

56 CRACKING UP
Page 83

ANSWER:
A CUCKOO CLUCK

57 END OF THE LINE
Page 86

ANSWER:
A STY SCRAPER
(skyscraper)

ALASK**A**

GLAS**S**
FAS**T**
TWENT**Y**

LES**S**
ATTI**C**
UNDE**R**
ASI**A**
STO**P**
FRE**E**
WINNE**R**

EVENING ROUND-UP

58 **COWS IN CLOVER**
Page 88

ANSWER:

. . . one in the GLOVE compartment.

The door won't CLOSE.

FIVE cows in your refrigerator.

There's an empty CONVERTIBLE parked out back.

Five cows in your OVEN.

59 **OPPOSITE DISTRACTION 1**
Page 89

ANSWER:

sADDLe
GOat
fLOCK
pONy
stALL
PASTure
stRAW

60 **RHODE ISLAND RED WORDS**
Pages 90-91

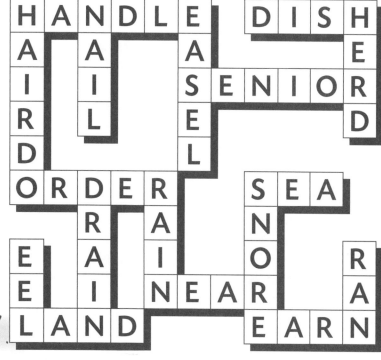

61 SICK DAZE
Page 92

ANSWER:
SHE HAD A VERY BAD COLT (cold).

62 LOVE LETTERS
Page 93

ANSWER:
A:3, B:4, C:5, D:1, E:2

A. **3**

B. **4**

C. **5**

D. **1**

E. **2**

63 MISSING IN ACTION
Pages 94-95

ANSWERS:

caBBAGe
sWEEt potato
caulifLOWer
aspaRAGus
squASH
BEEt
PEPper
carROT
LETtuce
sPINach

wATErmelon
apriCOT
hONEydew
pEAR
stRAWberry
oRANge
grAPE
TANgerine
cHERry

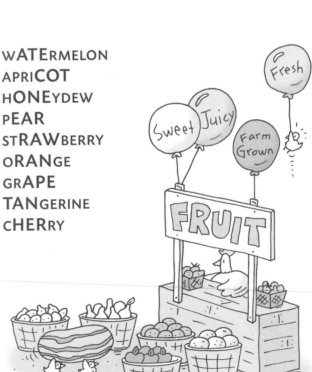

64 ROAD HOG
Page 96

ANSWER:
IN THE PORKING (parking) **LOT**

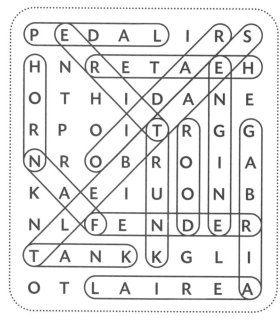

```
P E D A L I R S
H N R E T A E H
O T H I D A N E
R P O I T R G G
N R O B R O I A
K A E I U O N B
N L F E N D E R
T A N K K G L I
O T L A I R E A
```

65 DITCH DIGGERS
Page 97

FIELD

66 FAMILY TIES
Page 98

ANSWER:
MOTHER HEN

Meadow
Ocean
Tractor
Hawaii
Eraser
Rooster

Hawk
Earth
Nothing

67 IT'S ABOUT TIME
Page 99

ANSWER:
A NIGHT MARE

```
M O M E N T S A
I O E D A C E D
N N R I N W A D
U G H N A P S M
T T M Y I A O R
E W E E K N N E
D A Y V T R G T
R U O H E R A E
```

68 PICTURE CROSSWORD
Pages 100-101

69 FIVE BARNS
Page 102

70 ANNIE'S GRAM
Page 103

ANSWER:
CAT/ACT, ODE/DOE, OWL/LOW,
EWE/WEE, RAM/MAR, RAT/ART

OUR CAT MIGHT ACT FUNNY.

HE WROTE AN ODE TO HIS DOE.

THE OWL SLEEPS ON A LOW BEAM IN THE BARN.

THAT EWE IS WEE.

THE RAM CAN MAR LOTS OF THINGS.

I DREW A PICTURE OF A RAT IN MY ART CLASS.

71 I'VE GOT A CODE
Pages 104-105

ANSWERS:
Q: What do you call rows of cabbages?
A: Head lines!

Q: How do sheep fall asleep?
A: They count each other.

138

72 MIDDLE OF THE ROAD
Pages 106-107

ANSWERS:

THE COWROUSEL (carousel)   I AM A LITTLE HOARSE (horse)

maTch
usHer
crEep

baCon
brOom
toWel
thRee
brOwn
moUse
laSso
slEep
siLly

swIms

blAck
dIMes

scAle

jeLly
quIck
waTer
enTer
heLlo
quEen

asHes
clOwn
stAnd
maRch
paSte
swEet

73 TRUE/FALSE
Page 108

ANSWER:
PEN PALS

74 OPPOSITE DISTRACTION 2
Page 109

ANSWER:
PALomino
WETher
sWINe
sTALLion
SHEar
bILLy
INcubator

139

75 **WHO IS IT?**
Page 112

ANSWER:

Alphabetical Listing of Features

FOLLOW THE BOUNCING EGG

You can make your own animated movie!
Follow the 7 easy steps to make a rubber egg
bounce through the pages of this book.

1

Read all the directions
through once before starting.
The first step is to turn the
book sideways like this:

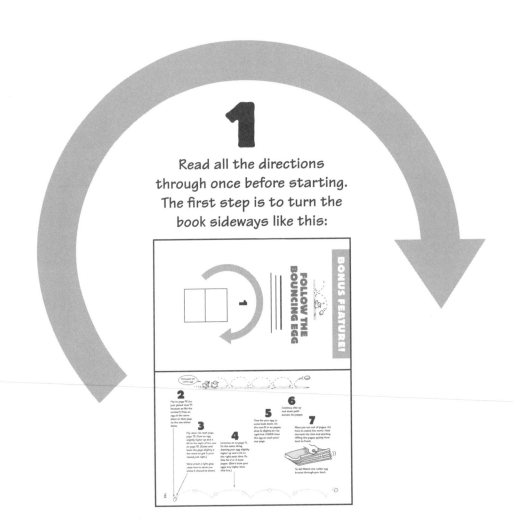

There goes the rubber egg!

2

Turn to page 75 (we just picked 75 because we like the number!) Draw an egg at the same place on that page as the one shown below.

3

Now turn to page 73. Draw an egg slightly higher up and a bit to the right of the one on page 75. (Raise and lower the page slightly a few times to get it positioned just right.)

We've drawn a light gray circle here to show you where it should be drawn.

4

Continue on to page 71. Do the same thing, drawing your egg slightly higher up and a bit to the right each time. Do this for 2 or 3 more pages. (Don't draw your eggs any higher than this line.)

5

Time for your egg to come back down. On the next 5 or so pages, draw it slightly to the right but LOWER than the egg on each previous page.

6

Continue this up and down path across the pages.

7

When you run out of pages, it's time to watch the movie. Hold the book like this and starting flipping the pages quickly from back to front:

Ta-da! Watch the rubber egg bounce through your book.

143

Other Storey Titles You Will Enjoy

Sea Life Games & Puzzles, by Cindy Littlefield. For all young fish fanatics, here is an irresistible collection of games, puzzles, trivia, riddles, brainteasers, and wit-sharpeners that will keep kids busy and entertained for hours at a time and in any location. 144 pages. Paperback. ISBN 1-58017-624-0.

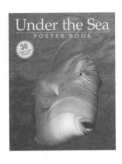

Under the Sea Poster Book. Bring the aquarium home with 30 full-color, pull-out portraits of fantastic sea creatures that kids love, plus plenty of fun facts that make each ocean resident unique and exciting. 64 pages. Paperback. ISBN 1-58017-623-2.

Horse Games & Puzzles for Kids, by Cindy Littlefield. More than 100 puzzles, activities, riddles, quizzes, and games to keep young horse-lovers happy and busy. 144 pages. Paperback. ISBN 1-58017-538-4.

Horses & Friends Poster Book. These 30 full-color posters feature horses with ponies, dogs, cats, goats, and other adorable companion animals. The irresistible posters are made for pulling out and decorating bedrooms, play rooms, lockers, or stables. 64 pages. Paperback. ISBN 1-58017-580-5.

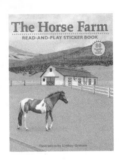

The Horse Farm Read-and-Play Sticker Book. Five full-color laminated horse environments are the blank canvases for hours of play with 80 reusable vinyl stickers. Text teaches the basics of equine care. 16 pages. Paperback. ISBN 1-58017-583-X.

The Horse Breeds Poster Book. Suitable for hanging on bedroom walls, in school lockers, or even in barns, these 30 posters show horses of all colors and sizes, at work, at play, and in competition. Facts about the pictured horse breeds are included on the back of each poster. 64 pages. Paperback. ISBN 1-58017-507-4.

The Petting Farm Poster Book. Thirty pull-out posters feature beautifully reproduced full-color images of chicks, ducklings, kids, lambs, calves, foals, piglets, rabbits, and more. The back of each poster contains fun facts about the animal's breed, habits, and history. 64 pages. Paperback. ISBN 1-58017-597-X.

These books and other Storey books are available wherever books are sold, or directly from Storey Publishing, 210 MASS MoCA Way, North Adams, MA 01247, or by calling 1-800-441-5700. Visit us at www.storey.com

144